v v v

Brushstrokes

v v v

Tom Boston

v v v

Cover background by Anna Ventura

Published by Allpoetry

General Synopsis

This book is truly a collection of eclectic poetry, ranging from a celebration of the seasons to a study of space. You will find within these pages, tales of travel, heartbreak and happiness; love songs and laments, laughter and tears. This is a book you can pick up at any time or place and find something to suit your mood.

About the Author

The author was born in Ireland and brought up in Brazil. He presently resides in the English Midlands. Poetry has been part of his life since being introduced to the works of Lord Byron by a friend in South America. The author began writing poetry as a means of channelling the passion and emotion of life into the written word. He often finds himself pondering the inexplicable and seeking the unobtainable. This reflects in his work.

Contents

Romance

Brushstrokes

Spring splashes colour on a landscape so bare.
The birdsong shrill fills the mild morning air.
Sun slivers slice through the leaves overhead
and tinge the dull greyness with brightness instead.

Light chases darkness and warmth blankets cold.
The new season emerges both busy and bold.
A new picture is painted in pigments so bright
toned by shy snowdrops in swathes of pure white.

Squirrels scuttle and peep from the tops of tall trees
as a sparrowhawk watches the dance of the bees.
Foxes and badgers forage, famished, for food,
while pigeon calls echo across the dense wood.

The rivers and meadows, the mountains and vales,
flaunt beauty and life as the winter's grip pales.
This mastery of nature, such talent, such flare.
Bold brushstrokes of colour on a canvas so bare.

A Vision Of Time

I see you clearly in a vision, sunlight shining on your face.
Reflecting youth and beauty, you're so happy in that place.
I call out through the mist of time but you are unaware.
As I reach for you, the vision fades, you are no longer there.

Ah, this enchanted place! How I hoped it was forever,
 but time fulfilled for both of us its merciless endeavour.
I try to grasp the ethereal bliss of a place that has passed by.
A silent scream forms on my lips but no one hears my cry.

I rage at the injustice of this stolen, priceless time.
My helplessness reminds me, it was borrowed, never mine.
Plans, regrets and wishes linger; wasted, barren in the past.
In that place where I just saw you, in the distance, oh so vast.

I must move on but long to stay so I might glimpse again,
that past we shared, that precious time, and there I would remain.
You did not see me gaze on you in that place without a care,
nor did you see me weep my love, for time we did not share.

The Seasons

I remember the warmth on my face,
touched by the rays of the Sun.
I remember the buds on the trees
and the promise of days full of fun.

I remember the bright blue skies
and the smell of fresh mown hay.
 I remember the glistening sea
and sails that luffed on their way.

I remember the tumbling leaves,
their scent and coloured fall.
I remember dull grey clouds,
the mist, the rain and the squall.

I remember the chill in the air,
the darkness, the ice and the snow.
I remember the cold, barren land
and a hearth with a welcoming glow.

Sleep

Awake, my love; my earnest prayer. I stand beside your tomb and stare.
Oh, that I could turn back the time to know you'd be forever mine.
Don't part from me. How can I bear to let you go and leave you there?

My heart accepts that you must go to that dark place we do not know
and there to hide from pain and toil and lie so still beneath this soil.
Rest now my dear, it's you laid low. You cannot share this bitter blow.

Go now from me. I shall not hear, again your laughter in my ear,
or share with you that zeal for life; the happiness, the times of strife.
Leave now my love and I'll wait here, in vain upon your grave to peer.

Fly now sweet soul, to heavens blue. Ascend forever from my view.
The passion, fervour and the zest no longer beat within your chest.
Repose in death; in life so true. This breathless form cannot be you.

Sleep now my love. I say farewell and none can fathom nor can tell
the void that your departure leaves or how my soul in anguish grieves.
Pass now my love, so cold, so pale, forever through the eternal veil.

Running With The J's

The wind-churned sea with leaps and peaks and lively twisting twirls,
moves to the fancy float and tune of a thousand dancing girls.
It spills and glints quicksilver-like and glimmers garnet green,
as the tips of tall trimmed sails appear in the distant hazy sheen.

Soon the mast is bearing down; keel slicing water through.
This mighty, splendid sailing boat holds to her course so true.
Tell-tails flying straight as dyes, she takes the centre-stage.
Her sleek hull lulls the wilding sea and dulls its noble rage.

As fabric flaps and halyards clap, she eases back from heeling.
She tacks her graceful bow away, with air from canvas peeling.
Sails spill the wind then fill again and shape like soaring wings
and through the surf she flows, she goes; her rigging loudly sings.

On the track of her new tack, she rides the raw emotion
of the frenzied, frothing, foaming sea, so graceful in her motion.
She charges, cutting up the waves and carves the ocean blue.
Through wind-blown swirls like dancing girls; a 'J' class and her crew.

Land Of My Youth

The long passage is ended; landfall awaits.
Lying at anchor at destiny's gates.
The scents, the sights and the sounds all around,
 are strange to me in this land we have found.

The sky a deep blue, the earth fiery red.
My senses are screaming inside my head.
The sands, the city and scenes fill my eyes.
Christ the Redeemer above all does rise.

Behind the first vision, forests I see,
like emeralds so green, reflecting the sea.
The shrills, the singing and samba I hear.
The language and lyrics, new to my ear.

The night air is filled with spice of this place.
The gentle sea breeze blows warm on my face.
The shacks, the shanties and shelters so small,
contrast with buildings so rich and so tall.

Diverse and exotic, this was to be
the land of my youth, a new home to me.

Sea Storm

At dawn this wild coast plays early host to a storm that's covered in cloud.
Waves rise and tumble and rolling they rumble under a low foggy shroud.
They froth and they hiss in a flurry of mist and carve their artwork on rocks.
They crash on the beach and threaten to breach walls protecting the docks.

Haze slowly lifts as the winds start to shift revealing the power of the Ocean.
Nautical surges bear down on sand verges reshaping land with their motion.
Swells rear and dip as a squall wields its whip and spurs white horses to run.
They thud on the coast with thunderous boast and a roar like a galleon's gun.

The storm on the Ocean, a sea in commotion spills onto a coastline so frail.
It's fickle and free and this treacherous spree strikes terror in those under sail.
Full of myth and magic, it's cruel and tragic; its splendour spans east to west.
Tides ebbing and flowing, ever coming and going; the Ocean is never at rest.

Far out to sea the storm rages free, forming peaks and canyons so grand.
Walls of water rise high to touch the grey sky and mock the mountains inland.
But the storm came and went, its venom is spent; the Ocean ran out of fight.
Now perfectly still like the pond of a mill; no waves or white horses in sight.

Kilravock

Amongst the granite and green, on an Oak tree I leaned
to rest in the shade of its crown.
For that moment just then, I was lord of this realm,
with these ruins of history renowned.
And in this ancient place, I tried to retrace
the footsteps of those from the past.
In that reticent wood, as a young man I stood
in search of the play's ghostly cast.

But none there was seen, not the Prince or the Queen
nor the Laird, named after the rose.
And the fierce men of war did battle no more.
No soldiers were railed against foes.
All the colours of fall seemed to recall
old memories from summers of lore.
The echoes of time and the ancient bells' chime
saluted a world that's no more.

Now, as I left this scene where legends have been,
I stole one more glance just to see,
if I only could glimpse that Queen or that Prince
or the soldiers that fought to be free.
The northern Sun teased its way through the leaves
and dappled the ground in its light,
And the tops of the trees, in tune with the breeze,
swayed as the crows took to flight.

*The author recalls a trip, as a young man, to Kilravock Castle (pronounced
Kilrock), Inverness, Scotland. The ancient home of the Roses or Rosses of*

Nairnshire who lived there in the 13th century. Famous visitors include Mary, Queen of Scots in 1562, Bonnie Prince Charlie (whom Sir Hugh Rose entertained with a violin rendition of an Italian minuet), the Duke of Cumberland (the day after the Prince's visit just before the two men fought the Battle of Culloden) and also the poet Robert Burns (in 1787).

Distant Shores

There is a land I want to show you, painting images to last.
I'll share with you its magic, charm and richness that is vast.
Fire red soil, its vibrant colour mixed with shades of vivid green.
Deep blue skies and shimmering waters of lagoons and lakes that gleam.

North to south stretch golden beaches where the rollers crash on sand.
Old towns and modern cities steal the earth where forests stand.
Southern mountains rise in splendour with their woods of evergreen
looking almost 'out of place' in this warm sub-tropic scene.

In the centre of this country where plantations meet demand,
coffee, sugar and much more, mean trees are giving way to land.
Muddy rivers flow through greenery, twist and splinter into   streams.
Slowly downwards they meander through the regions yet unseen.

To the north there stands a forest, it's the Amazon by name.
Brazil's own precious Eden; promised land of worldwide fame,
with exotic vegetation, where the jaguar skulks and roams
and the ancient tribal nations build their sun-baked earthen homes.

My hope is if you've never been to see this wonderland,
these words I've penned inspire you to, then you will understand
my passion for those distant shores and why they make me yearn
and why the memories of this place entice me to return.

Sunsets Of Red

The Sun is like silver arrayed in the sky
and contrasts with blue like a Far Eastern dye.
The rivers run clear as a cold mountain spring.
The air fills with arias as the summer birds sing.

Trees spread their boughs in deep shades of green
and flower petals paint an impressionist scene.
The grass sways and dances in the breath of a breeze
as the butterflies float with fairy-like ease.

The bees make their honey while ants stock their nest.
A woodpecker's pecking wakes the squirrels' rest.
The silver and blue shimmer bright overhead
with a warm summer's promise and sunsets of red.

Space and Time

Priceless

From the beginning she was there.
For mortal man she has no care.
When at our end for life we plead,
she will not hear, she cannot heed.

The Great may offer gold as pay.
To sup on life for one more day.
But at the last roll of the dice,
she won't be bought; she has no price.

This precious gift so soon is past.
Like fickle flames too spent to last
or flowers cut down in perfect prime.
She is our Mistress, she is Time.

Space

What is this expanse where darkness dwells?
This space unknown that answers to no name.
No meaning can describe its perfect awe,
nor reason can expound its shrouded fame.

This eternal mass, though mass it cannot be,
nor can it be a void for it holds all things within.
An endless abyss, where chaos forms its laws.
Limitless, timeless, time too is trapped therein.

Its darkness tames the fury of a flaming Sun
and quells the stars, as sparks 'neath water plunged.
Their light, their heat, their power, their all,
drawn into its blackness and there expunged.

It clasps all things inside its frigid grip.
All grandeur shrinks and pales in this expanse.
Yet fragile life is found in its embrace.
A universe preserved; defended, takes her stance.

Does it exist to shield this dawn of life
and cocoon her like a rare and precious stone?
In this fearful, dreadful span she hides.
This diverse place, unique and on her own.

Is this dark vastness solely there to frame
the possession of an unseen higher force?
Such greatness is beyond the human mind.
Can we begin to fathom this enigmatic source?

What is this expanse where darkness dwells?
Where time did never bloom nor know decay.
Did it begin and will it end or can we know
its Alpha and Omega; its first and final day?

Apocalyptic

The Voice

I heard a lament like the wind in the trees;
the voice of a spirit, so faint in the breeze.
As the spectre drew closer it began to foretell,
the world that sustains us would soon be our hell.

Of the oceans it spoke, no life in their reaches.
No tides ebb and flow; no waves on the beaches.
Great forests destroyed; hacked down for the land.
Deserts so barren where woods used to stand.

It wept for the earth exposed to the Sun,
scorched and parched where rivers did run.
For the famished and plagued and wars that they fight;
for the slaughter and waste; the hatred and spite.

The day of reckoning it promised soon
when twilight will dim the stars and the moon.
In a vision it showed the last of our race,
stood huddled and wretched in that final place.

For daylight they waited but the dawn didn't rise.
In darkness they squinted through non-seeing eyes.
They shrieked as they learnt that the end had begun
and cursed their existence for what they had done.

Masters Of Fire

At the dawn of mankind, men lived on their own,
hunting and gathering with tools made of bone.
Tribes began forming and language emerged
and nations were born as people converged.

The Masters of Fire now divided by borders,
each had their rules, their leaders and orders.
But it wasn't enough, they needed a cause
to protect their traditions, lifestyle and laws.

Doctrines and dogmas began to appear,
subduing the masses through fables and fear.
And the gods they created could not stand alone.
Lifeless and powerless; crafted from stone.

They prayed to idols they knew couldn't speak
but humanity worshipped because it was weak.
And the tenets of faith were always to blame
for the evil committed in their deity's name.

Down through the ages the nations have travelled.
History repeating as the centuries unravelled.
Warring and sacking since man's early time,
with each faction asserting approval divine.

Religion and temples and the cities they built
won't afford them protection from wages of guilt.
The 'Masters of Fire' are the gods of their fate.
Will they learn from their past before it's too late?

The Dark

Darkness was all. She was absolute; the Mistress of all that exists.
And Darkness ceded to the Sun and Moon so night and day were born.
Each day light dulled so feeble fire flamed life and lit the ways of men.
She could command all light and the might of ten-thousand suns
or as a spark suppressed, this light would universal lightlessness become.

Heat and power both perish in her grasp; she has no use for them.
Yet out of Darkness all that was and is became. Galaxies and planets
with their spinning moons, bask but for a moment in the glow of stars.
Their Mistress bides her time and in her patient sojourn, life converged.
Clasping to her darkened hem, child-like into lended light it did emerge.

Fretful, fragile, futile life, fearful of the dimming and descent to dark.
Millennia mass and melt as centuries chase across her dark domain.
Darkness is eternal and so she waits. She waits and knows not time.
Time, the maker of mortals and mocker of men, to her it holds no sway.
It flows and ebbs and flows again, whilst she keeps the light at bay.

But Darkness will rouse one awful day. She will rise and rest no more.
Fires will no longer kindle life nor burning lights light up these realms.
Earth and its borrowed time will flee with faint-lit stars into her depths.
Suns will shrink and freeze and spinning moons will slow and stall.
Life's lease so brief and now extinct; perfect in her desolation, Darkness
is all.

War

The March

They marched in peace for their rights to insist,
but the army went in to make them desist.
The crack of their rifles, flash of their guns,
mowed down without warning fathers and sons.

White flags were flown but they soon turned to red.
People knelt down by the dying and dead.
The troops looked on and some were bemused;
others, bewildered at how they'd been used.

"For Queen and Country" was their battle cry.
A war machine trained and ready to die.
Their campaigns and conquests, colours so grand.
Just butchers that day in this troubled Land.

Then came the revenge, that awful death blow.
Man's hatred for man; no mercy on show.
All blown to pieces with ear-splitting thud.
Young soldiers left strewn and dying mud.

And so, the war divided this nation.
Loathing and spite defied explanation.
Slaughter and suffering, the terrible cost.
No victors or gain, just lives that were lost.

Castles

On a cold February morning the lakes full and overflowing were writhing and rippling; stirred by an icy gale. The waters tumble, twist, rush and babble on their way.

We stand on hallowed ground, surrounded by nature's beauty so wild so pure, it stills all other sound so we may hear the haunting tones of history whispering in the wind of sacred ancient times.

This is a land of legends, a realm of Keeps and Kings where ethereal waters shimmer in the winter sunlight and
guard Erne's secrets in their darkest depths.

We leave this sainted soil to walk upon more recent plots. No ancient relics here but mortar, brick, and slate decayed. Silent barren dwellings; here too history has a say.

No battlements rise or ramparts stand on these forgotten fertile lots. Here no Viking came to plunder nor Earl rose up to flee the land. No forts, no feuds; just humble homesteads battle time.

These little homes once splendid in their purpose. A noble cause of grateful hearts. From those that stayed in peace and lived, to these who went and warred and all but died.

To save the shreds of these torn lives, lives splintered by the shells and shards of war. Shattered, battered remnants of men who stared at death yet dared not die.

This is our history, time and pain. Blood that in our veins flows now, flowed free from theirs on Flanders fields.
Touched by death on poppied planes they died in part and there lie still.

Have we so soon forgotten, leaving memories to decay? And are the valiant deeds of those so young, so bold now turned to dust and scattered like these small abodes?

These symbols signs of peace and hope. Tokens to our fellow man now slowly tumble into earth and there to
waste like friend and foe on no man's land.

These piles, these ruins, these wrecks, these heaps of broken stone, were castles once to these brave men.

Lines written following a visit to the remains of eleven picturesque cottages, built on Cleenish Island, Lough Erne, Ireland, just after the Great War. They were provided at low rent, together with a plot of land each (thirty to forty acres), to eleven chosen survivors and heroes of that conflict. They are now in a serious state of disrepair. This region is steeped in history and mysticism. Truly inspirational; a poet's dream.

The Somme

Eruptions like thunder ripped through the air;
the fright the dread and the cries of despair.
Cowering in corners men sought out cover.
Others penned words of farewell to a lover.
 Some just laid low in the soil and the mud,
in the hope of escaping each shattering thud.

The smoke billowed thickly, drifting and grey,
hiding the bodies heaped up where they lay.
Shells fell like rain on the lines of defence.
Utter destruction, so vile so intense.
The barrage fell silent with the last round.
Survivors crawled out from under the ground.

Across No Man's Land ranks started to cheer,
assured their assault was nothing to fear.
"Just a leisurely walk", the soldiers were told.
They'd no way of knowing what would unfold.
The orders came down to start the advance
and young men obeyed, as if in a trance.

The spearhead went first; all seemed to go well.
Then guns opened up; men staggered and fell.
The hail of fire in a short space of time,
cut that generation down in its prime.
Mothers and daughters in vain they did pray,
for the fathers and sons slaughtered that day.

Fighting and firing at long last did cease.
Only in death did the fallen find peace.
The price was so high that they had to pay.
The cost to them was a grave in that clay.
The warring, the killing and carnage is gone.
Just rows of white crosses and memories live on.

Fields Of Wheat And Barley

On this isle of laughter and legend,
where the shades of green softly taint
the summer so long,
with praise and with song,
in the land of the scholar and saint.
And the preachers preached to the just men
as the wrong men fought in their prime,
to a tune that was sung for a Dutchman to come,
through the valleys of ages and time.

And for the people divided by singing,
the music turned peace into war.
Through long shining days,
in oblivion it played,
unaware of the winter in store.
In a country where hedgerows and ditches,
full of berries and blackbirds in song,
framed the gold fields of wheat and of barley,
in that summer that lasted so long.

But as long as it was, it came to a close,
and a chilled, callous winter took hold.
And rivers and streams
washed away my young dreams,
as wavering warmth turned to cold.
I could not understand this curse on my land,
I was too young to harbour belief.
In the last of the green, where summer had been,
there I quickly grew up to know grief.

The wrong and the just and the preachers they trust,
sowed seeds of cold discontent.
The whirlwind they reaped,
the hatred they heaped
was the harvest of evil they meant.
And the barley and wheat were scorched in the flame;
by bullets and bombs set alight.
For the Dutchman's creed, how this island did bleed,
in that cold, cruel winter's long night.

Set in the late Sixties, the author uses metaphorical language to lament an idyllic childhood, tainted by the civil war in Ireland. A war simply known as "The Troubles".

Knights Of The Sky

The enemy stood eager and poised at our door,
awaiting the order to invade our free shore.
Just a strip of blue sea kept the foe from our land
and above it, the skies where we made our stand.

To like-minded free nations we sent out our call.
They offered their service, their lives and their all.
This was not their home but the cause was the same.
For freedom to fight, in their hundreds they came.

They arrived from all over to repel the advance
of an empire of evil and deny it the chance
of suppressing this bastion's freedom of speech
and enslaving the nations within its long reach.

These knights of the sky were our heroes of lore;
just a sheepskin jacket, the armour they wore.
Their colours, a roundel on a background of blue.
Their swords were the wings of the aircraft they flew.

Their steeds were the planes that they rode in the skies.
They flew for freedom and they flew for their lives.
Each day they did battle they knew they might die.
But still these young heroes were willing to fly.

For almost four months they fought and they died.
With our native pilots they flew side by side.
Against all the odds we defeated that power,
and this was, without question, their finest hour.

When we look to the sky above our free land,
we salute those young knights for service so grand.
Free nations worldwide shall be ever in debt
and those bravest of men, they will never forget.

Unknown Warrior

Private A, the baker's son, is having one last smoke
with private B, the draper's boy, an all-round decent bloke.
Then there's private C, the vicar's younger brother
and private D who's terrified and wants to run for cover.

Private E writes to his lass, while F writes to his Dad
and private G's as bold as brass, though he is just a lad.
H, the one that gives the orders, he knows oh so well,
the order he's about to give will send them into hell.

Too soon the soldiers hear the call; a whistle to advance.
The baker's son and all his mates step up with death to dance.
From A to Z, their fate is sealed; the massacre goes on.
The draper's boy, the vicar's kin and private D all gone.

A soldier lay in no-man's land whose story we don't know.
He fought with friends and strangers and bravely faced the foe.
He fell with them in Flanders fields, a warrior with no name.
With Kings and Queens he lies at rest; in death he has found fame.

Political

Royal Service

The Emperor King now lies in state,
life's toil and duty done.
The nobles of this land file past.
These nations mourn as one.

The young Princess assumes the throne,
with grit and faith renowned.
And so, in June of fifty-three,
this Royal brow was crowned.

The burden passed to one so young,
from Princess to be Queen.
And thus, began the longest reign
this realm has ever seen.

The Commonwealth so vast, so far.
Its subjects celebrate
the passion and the love displayed
by our new Head of State.

The world has seen much change in time.
Its leaders waxed and waned.
Through turmoil and uncertain times,
our Kingdom has remained.

God save our noble, gracious Queen,
our earnest supplication.
In thankfulness we bow the knee
with pride and admiration.

The People's Choice

The People grumbled at the federal dream.
Whispers and rumours started to stream.
The stream, now a torrent, would not go away,
so, the Government thought we should all have a say.

The Lib Dems reacted and called for a vote.
Labour agreed, so they'd not miss the boat.
Two camps emerged, leave and remain.
The Nation divided, under great strain.

The electorate was told it had just this chance
to decide on its future by taking a stance.
"We'll honour the verdict, we'll do as you say,"
the People were told, before the big day.

Promises were easy, they thought we'd all stay.
Then shock and horror, as most walked away.
"The result is not binding," they cried from the floor,
but the masses had spoken as never before.

To compromise, a new choice was invented.
A hard or soft Brexit, if it can't be prevented.
And so, the Remainers, with all of their might,
campaigned to stay and readied to fight.

"The public were not in possession of facts,"
said they, as they offered numerous pacts.
"Vote one more time and make the correction."
The People said "no, but we'd like an election."

"We'll have no election," the Remainers did say,
"until a deal is obtained before exit day."
A deal was secured, and brought back to the House.
"But we want further measures," they started to grouse.

They tried to delay through a dubious pact,
as they clung to the Fixed Term Parliament Act.
But they knew, in the end, that their days were numbered.
Departure from Europe would not be encumbered.

The Public had spoken, but they spoke once again,
when they got their election and showed their disdain.
For Parliament's palter and a man-made disaster,
the members were punished by the People, their master.

The Leave camp assured us that sovereign we'll be.
We've now left the Union, they say we are free.
Success or failure, in the future now stands.
The Nation's new destiny lies in our hands.

Lines To A Modern Empire

Leave the land that you've invaded,
sheltered there you should not be.
Yours, a land of culture barren;
throneless, heartless tyranny.

Ours a Kingdom forged by conflict;
born within and from the sea.
An envied charter, won by courage,
fairness, speech and liberty.

Ours an empire, flawed and fractious,
spanned the earth from east to west.
Giving birth to powerful nations
where freedom beats in every chest.

Yours an empire built on avarice,
grasping power with heavy hand.
Plundering in the name of justice
with contempt an ancient land.

The Politician

Some politicians of today have lost their purpose and their way.
Passion is no longer chief; they do not hold to their belief.
You pay their fee and take your choice, for silver they will be your voice.
They'll fight for you if you've got gold; beware they can be bought and sold.

They'll make a speech and take an oath then turn a devious back on both.
Truth and lies are what they sell, they have no preference which they tell.
When it gets tough, they'll turn their coat; they'll stop at nothing for your vote.
They've never worked or held a job; they love the rich, the poor they rob.

They never ever speak their mind; to most injustice they are blind.
They'll tell you what you want to hear and then deny it out of fear.
They represent you day by day but really don't deserve their pay.
Professionals with no conviction, that's today's new politician.

Fantasy

Evergreen Wood

Two figures make their way across the pine-needled ground of a dark, dark evergreen wood. Shadow-like they go.
They flow, as ghosts and move as spirits move; like spectres, yet they breathe.
And with each breath they breathe, they're filled with the earthy essence of the evergreen.
Musty mildew on bits of bark, and fungus covered fallen firs, fused with perfumed pine.

And the woodland softly sleeps. Its slumber split by the screechy scream of a distant fox and the haunting hoot of a hunting owl, flying phantom-like, from bough to bough.
The two press on with perfect purpose, tramping tough terrain. Slowly through the dark they move.
A light appears in another time, and then, it's gone. At the very time it goes, it glows, above the wood.

The figures halt and through the trees they gaze and raise their eyes perplexed.
Transfixed towards the sky they stare and dare not move, stricken beneath this foreign orb.
The moon, wrapped in drapes of darkened cloud now wakes while stars keep watch and yield.
Wolves howl then whimper and flocks of wakened birds take fright and flap in frantic fear.

The light grows closer, brighter, bolder as it moves mute across the sky.
It flashes thrice and then,

as though a switch were flicked, it's gone. The dim draped moon resumes its sleep as darkness now descends. They wonder what it is they've seen and where it went and why and sense they're not alone. In the shadows stands a figure and they, first bewildered then bewitched, hear what it has to say.

Without speech it speaks and without speech they listen. No voice disturbs the dormant wood.
It steals into their minds and makes them see the mysteries of the stars and suns revealed.
How man one day will tame light's speed and tether thought and by that tether conquer time.
It speaks of distant planets, of other worlds and far-flung moons just a dream, a thought away.

At the speed of thought the light returned turns night to day. They watch. They wait. They wait.
For this descendent demi-god they wait. In vain they look for more from this enlightened erudite.
Darkness falls again. They search the shadows, seeking, sensing and sense this time they are alone. The night settles into slumber.
The moon and stars from cloudy cover creep and sleep no more.

The wood whiff drifts on the dank breeze. Musky mould and pungent pine permeate the twilight. A fox-shriek mingles with the hoot-hooting of a hunting owl slipping swiftly tree to tree.
Shadows grow in the undraped moonlight. Ghost-like they grow in the glow of meandering stars.
Two figures make their way across the pine-needled ground of the dark, dark evergreen wood.

Lines written following the sighting in the sky of an unidentified object by the author's younger daughter. The author indulges in a little bit of reality-inspired fantasy. Here we accompany two characters, who having experienced an 'Encounter of the Fifth kind', as they say, are left bewildered. The context and content of the last verse is perhaps suggesting that the two figures are left wondering if they have imagined the whole thing.

Bygone Sea

Now, as I walk upon this sand and etch the water's edge
with every footstep that I take, I make myself a pledge.
I swear that I shall leave the land to sail away once more.
I close my eyes and start to dream and let my spirit soar.

And as I fly across the waves to see what I can see.
The ghosts of ancient sailors are looking up at me.
I see the white sails luffing in a stiffening breeze,
sun-bleached decks and mighty masts that once were living trees.

Merchant ships and little ships and flagships of the line,
toast the spirits of the sea with the fruit of vine.
A schooner passes on its way on course for foreign land.
Its rigging set and singing loud to Neptune's merry band.

Humpback whales come up to breathe as dolphins leap nearby.
Searching seabirds skim through waves and longful seagulls cry.
Fishing boats with jolly crews haul in one last net.
With bilges full they head for home, with all their canvas set.

Too soon my spirit scoops the wind and sails into the sky.
As I look down, this ghostly seascape starts to pass me by.
And so, these ancient sailors, their shanties and their tales, begin to fade.
My dream is gone; reality prevails.

As I stroll back along the coast and leave this white-capped sea,
I know these salty bygone days are where I long to be.

Contact

In a distant part of space, where time does not hold sway,
spinning moons and searing suns make up night and day.
Prancing stars, another Mars and comets yet unseen,
dance to a tune unknown to man, in space he's never been.
Other life forms, far advanced, share peacefully this place
and moons ago, the speed of light was broken by this race.
To any sphere away from here by thought alone they go,
confusing laws of physic, they defy all that we know.
So, if you take a stroll at night, lit by the moon and stars
you just might glimpse a flying craft that isn't one of ours.
What they see in you and me, is hardly worth a mention.
Still, they come and visit us from their own dimension.

The Vagrant

As I wandered through the quiet streets, carefree in the night,
skulking shadows swayed around me in the dimming light.
Amongst these shifting shapes, I saw the figure of a man,
as I passed by, he reached and caught me gently by the hand.

Despite his tattered clothing and the cardboard for his bed,
something drew me to this stranger, then this is what he said:
"Would you pause with me one moment, sir, to look back over time,
at things that shaped the lives of men, including yours and mine?"

So, I took a break from walking and sat down on the ground -
just me and this mysterious man with no one else around.
He beckoned with his hand to draw me closer so I'd hear.
Then he began to speak and show me scenes from yesteryear.

I saw three men of evil spread death where 'er they went.
Evil empires they created; their power is long since spent.
Millions died in their arenas, in their cruel wicked games.
What if these three had never lived and no one knew their names?

Next, I saw three men of peace who wrought for all mankind.
Their sacrifice and early deaths consumed my fevered mind.
For emancipation, human rights and freedom they campaigned.
What if they'd lived their lives in full with all their goals attained?

The final vision shown to me was a battle fought between
three angels and three demons, so I asked what did it mean.
"Was this just myth or legend or a doomsday revelation?"
He turned to me and with a smile, he gave this explanation:

"The angels are man's virtues; honour, courage and compassion.
The demons are his shame, his fears and lack of human passion.
This battle represents man's choice to follow either way.
When leaders of our World choose evil, mankind has to pay"

I turned to face this stranger to enquire how he had planted
in my mind, the things I saw and things I took for granted.
The cardboard and a ragged coat were all that could be seen.
This homeless man had somehow gone, as though he'd never been.

So, I walked on slowly through the streets of this old lonely place
and pondered on the night's events and the choices that we face.
Man's foibles and his virtues, good and evil, peace or death
and I wondered who this vagrant was who vanished in a breath.

Red And Gold

Who is that girl with fire red hair,
seen walking through the valley there?
She glides each day across the meadow,
through a sea of flowers bright yellow.

She sings a song with a voice so sweet
and moves so lightly on her feet.
There is no trail where she has been,
no footprints on the ground are seen.

This siren with her hair of flame.
No one knows from whence she came.
Her timeless tune bewitches men
but she remains aloof from them.

Through ages she's remained unknown,
walking through these blooms alone.
Who is this girl from times of old,
with fire red hair and dress of gold?

Miscellaneous

Lesson For Life

The mistress burns the midnight oil, her lessons to prepare.
Her charges slumber in their beds, snug and unaware.

Then at dawn, a new day starts and early in the morning,
the mistress leaves to go to school, toast in hand and yawning.

Through the school-gates she arrives and hurries to the class,
her noisy chatting students make room to let her pass.

She takes her place; the lesson starts. The chatter has abated
and slowly homework is produced; some of it belated.

Textbooks opened on the desks, the mistress starts to teach
with dedication to the class and targets they must reach.

The mistress knows it's up to her to tutor each with zest
and fill her pupils with the need to do their very best.

If she succeeds to teach each one and for their future strives,
then part of her will stay with them throughout their adult lives.

Winter

Winter, frigid winter! How I loathe this wretched season.
Dullness, greyness, leaflessness. I cannot see the reason,
why we should suffer every year the misery that it brings.
The cold, the wet, the long dark nights and other hateful things.

Winter, barren winter! How I loathe this awful time.
Dampness, sickness, lifelessness. I could cope just fine,
if it only lasted for a month instead of three or four.
The frost, the slush, the sleety rain. I cannot take much more.

Winter, fleeting winter, will soon give way to spring.
Brightness, gladness, leafiness; the joys that it will bring.
A few more weeks of misery, as winter follows fall,
so that which follows winter will rejuvenate us all.

The Child

A little child held out his hand as if for coin to plea.
But I passed by this little one pretending not to see.
His saddened eyes looked up at me and I looked down at him.
With matted hair and tattered clothes and fragile frame so thin.

I hurried on into my day, for money isn't free.
I told myself I couldn't stop; there's somewhere I must be.
But the memory of that tiny face refused to leave my mind.
I turned and walked back to that spot the little one to find.

The rich in cars clog up the streets, they queue for love of gold.
Merchants count their profits from all the goods they've sold.
Well-dressed people walk the parks, their wealth is plain to see.
I wonder if they saw the child and walked on just like me.

The child had gone I'd missed my chance, I wouldn't get another.
Was this boy alone on Earth, no friend, no kin or mother?
The image of him standing there, haunts me to my shame.
This child belongs to all of us though we don't know his name.

Wild River

The river through the forest seeps,
it twists and turns; it runs, it creeps.
It's free and mad and wildling wild,
it's rough at times, at times it's mild.

It rushes past tall leaning trees,
gushing through the gorge it flees.
Picking up the pace it goes,
this savage river widening flows.

It froths and foams towards the sound
of crashing water smashing ground.
At the edge its canter stalls
then launching headlong, down it falls.

The torrent carves an ancient pool
in shades of green so deep, so cool
and misty spray with its chill blow
refreshes ferns that round it grow.

And from that pool a trickle spills;
it gathers pace, it floods, it fills.
It twists and turns; it swells it swirls.
The river's might again unfurls.

Need To Know

Man needs a creator, a better, a maker
and belief in a force that's infinitely greater.
Man needs a power to blame for his ailing,
to justify actions and account for his failing
Many believe after life comes infinity
and in an omniscient eternal divinity.

The belief in a deity is one that persists.
Believers by faith accept God exists.
Now belief without proof may seem a bit odd,
but then so does the outright denial of God.
Some say that denial is just as absurd
as praying to God and not being heard.

Despite his beliefs man still strives to know
who and what are we and where we will go.
Maybe the reason we inhabit this place
can only be known by the author of Space.
Mankind has a burning desire to find out
its purpose, its source or what life is about.

Lines To My Children

My children hear me speak to you.
My time on Earth is halfway through.
I've made mistakes along life's road.
I've been neglectful truth be told.
The nest you've left and flown away
Please listen to what I must say.

This is your time, your day, your space.
This is your realm, your world, your place
Live life so full, live life with love.
Your limit is the sky above.
Love what you do and who you're with,
for life is real it's not a myth.

Travel far and travel wide.
Keep prudence always by your side.
Chase your dreams and fight your fights.
Honour justice and guard your rights.
Defend the weak, support the sick.
To wrath and anger be not quick.

Be humble in your own success.
Avoid the pitfall of excess.
Take pride in everything you do.
Despise what's false, embrace what's true.
My children hear these words I plead.
Follow them and you'll succeed.

A Call To Write

The art of writing poetry,
is not an art to me.
It's something that we all can do.
Try and you will see.
The power of pen on paper
and of thoughtful written lines,
can entertain and thrill our hearts
and open up our minds.

Lightless

Oh darkness to your cover, in the night I flee.
The pain, again, it seeks me out; so dark I cannot see.
My struggle to stay sane is overwhelmed by sadness.
Each day I stray a little more into the realm of madness.

At night my silent plight I fear, alone in this dark place.
I stare at barren emptiness; no comfort in this space.
My soul, it longs for morning light as I lay wide awake.
Relief I seek each waking hour from this constant ache.

And daytime slowly lingers, towards its baleful eve.
No comfort can I find in things that once I did believe.
I strive against the looming cold and dusk of grey twilight.
Darkness, come to me again; tomorrow I must fight.

Humour

The Piglet And The Bear

Pooh Bear went to Piglet's house to tell him of his plan.
When he heard it, Piglet knew that he was not Pooh's man.
"An adventure we are going to have," the bear said to his friend.
But the little pig was thinking then, "this friendship ought to end."

Piglet was convinced by Pooh; they made the bravest pair.
So off they went, the two of them; the piglet and the bear.
They came across a tree which the two pals walked around.
Then Piglet froze in horror. There were footprints on the ground.

He didn't mind a walk with Pooh or a gentle little trot,
but the thought of footprints round the tree, he didn't like a lot. Pooh
Bear reassured his chum that they should see this through.
While Piglet quickly called to mind a dozen things to do.

"You may or may not know this," said Pooh to his wee mate.
"We'll have to hunt and trap these things, before it is too late."
Piglet jumped and skipped with fear, his little eyes grew wide.
Pooh was getting worried too, but hid it due to pride.

Around the tree they slowly crept, with Piglet very troubled.
And then he nearly fainted 'cos the footprints had now doubled.
Every time they went around, more footprints did appear.
By now the little piglet chap was paralysed with fear.

"Heffalumps we're hunting here," said Pooh Bear sounding tough.
But the truth was, just like Piglet, Pooh too had had enough.
And so, the story goes, my dears; a hunt by two great friends.
If you haven't read the books by now, you'd better make amends.

Middle-Aged Chap's Christmas

Here's what we want
from Santa this year.
We long for flat stomachs,
despite too much beer.

A thick head of hair,
like a rock 'n' roll King,
and trousers so tight,
they'd positively ping.

We want our old memory
and vigour of youth
and to chew on pork scratchings
without breaking a tooth.

We'd love our old wardrobe
to fit once again;
to wear a size medium
without crippling pain.

We'd like to be carefree,
trendy and cool,
instead of becoming
an old-fashioned fool.

Not fat and grumpy
or too fond of bed
or covered in hair
that should be on one's head.

We won't get our wishes
and neither will you.
Santa's a sadist
and Christmas is blue.

We can try to be good
and write him a letter,
in the slim hope the old boy
will make us look better.

On the morning of Christmas
we know when we rise,
the mirror won't greet us
with a sight for sore eyes.

So, season's greetings
to you and your kin
and try to accept
your new double chin.

Lockdown

Lockdown again.
Oh, what a pain!
This virus is driving me mad.

Too much Tv,
with nothing to see.
Online is now just as bad.

The Chancellor is spending
amounts never ending,
in a vain bid to keep us afloat.

The PM is flagging,
his hairdo is sagging.
It's starting to get on his goat.

To add to our misery
and this is so grisly.
The US has voted once more.

The choice was appalling.
Their standard is falling.
An old guy or same as before.

The votes were recounted
as a protest was mounted.
They tried to deny the election.

They became so abusive,

but results were conclusive.
In part we can thank this infection.

So, try to remember,
that nothing's forever.
The threat of Corona will cease.

And life will get better
with no viral fetter;
with mankind and nature at peace.

Winter Rain

About winter rain, I do complain
and fittings without fixtures.
A dusty home and missing comb
and walls with wonky pictures.

Dirty cars and 'jumped up stars'
who think they are God's gift.
Noisy kids, ill-fitting lids,
are things that get me miffed.

Traffic lights and cancelled flights
and zips that won't do up.
These are things that bother me,
like wine served in a cup.

Holey socks and mental blocks,
the internet offline.
Untidy rooms and misplaced brooms,
and running out of time.

Keys I've lost, the flipping cost
of heating oil and gas.
Dogs that bark, no space to park,
are things that I find crass.

Bulbs that blow and names that go,
that I should still remember.
Shops that start their Christmas season
early in September.

And so, the list goes on, my friends,
but I need to end this caper.
It's not the lack of inspiration.
I'm running out of paper.

Hot And Cold

Wonderland and no-man's land, both places we have been.
Sunshine mixed with rainfall, is something we've all seen.
Waterfalls in desert sands; a nomad's great relief.
Faith and doubt together; the basis for belief.

Love and dreaded hatred, make uneasy fellows.
Temper and tranquillity, as a person mellows.
War and peace, I have to add; a clichéd combination.
Feast and famine shouldn't happen; not in any nation.

Synonyms and antonyms. Terms that do oppose.
Words that rhyme and words that don't; poetry and prose.
Promised land or hell on Earth, I'm in writer's heaven.
Ten antipodes I've listed here, or maybe there's eleven.

A Hundred Peas

A hundred peas or thereabouts,
heaped on my plate but I have doubts
about the way they should be eaten.
By this legume, I won't be beaten.

I might use a pin and try
to prick each one before I die.
Or maybe I should use a spoon.
That way I'm bound to finish soon.

Perhaps I'd better use my knife.
These blessed peas aren't worth the strife.
But here's a little tip for you
and this is what you ought to do.

Treat them like you would a flan
and place cooked peas into a pan.
Whisked egg then goes in the mix.
Your pea dilemma this will fix.

Like an omelette gently cook.
Then grill the top and take a look.
The peas now trapped will not escape.
Just slice and serve it like a cake.

The Paradox Of Irony

Umbrellas in the desert, snowshoes in the sand.
Playing with two fingers on a baby grand.
If you want to live in peace you must prepare for battle.
Why are some snakes camouflaged if they have a rattle?

Starlight when we see it, has long ago extinguished.
People in disguises often look distinguished.
Oil and water never mix, like calmness and emotion.
Then tell me what emulsion is, explain to me this potion.

Fishermen, when in the bar, have only caught huge fish.
Throwing coins in fountains, if money is your wish.
Can you see the irony or the paradox explain?
Or have these lines of poetry been written all in vain?

The Expert

If you're in a hot debate
and deem that you are right,
and think the other person
isn't quite so bright.
Just take care and be aware
that you may have to yield.
You might find you are talking to
an expert in their field.

Leaving Home

The kids grew up and left our home,
it took me by surprise.
I thought they'd stay forever,
beneath our watchful eyes.
I wander down to empty rooms
and peer in through the door
and wonder where they are right now
and what life has in store.

Chilled Out

The fridge is very useful
for keeping fresh food chilled.
But ours is full of ancient things
and sauces that have spilled;
crummy butter, rancid milk
and ham that's out of date.
The only stuff that's fit to eat
are things that we all hate.

Lines To My Lover

I met you in the summer of nineteen eighty-four.
I took a trip to Inverness where I'd never been before.
I went to see the castle and meet some Scottish folk,
but I suspect that you went there, to meet the perfect bloke.

You marked me out and kept me far from all the competition,
then you worked your charm on me like someone on a mission.
I didn't know what hit me, I didn't stand a chance,
you bowled me over, stole my heart, and led me on a dance.

You had the sweetest face I'd seen, with Janice Joplin hair,
knitted tops and matching beads meant we were soon a pair.
Those little shoes you used to wear, with smooth tanned legs to boot.
I couldn't take my eyes of you because you were so cute.

Thirty-seven years have passed; we've had our share of fights,
I love you just as much as then, despite your knitted tights.
Your beads no longer match, my dear, in fact, they're never worn
and your nylons, full of ladders, are almost always torn.

Five kids on we're still a team; a real successful mix.
I wrote these lines for you because today you're fifty-six.
So, I wish you happy birthday - don't let this cause a rift,
I confess I wrote this poem for you 'cos I forgot your gift.

Desperation

I sit here thinking what to write and wonder if I'll see the light
of an idea that I can use, from any source or recent news.
I hold my head in desperation and wait in vain for inspiration.
Even staying up at night, the page is blank, try as I might.

At times like these I scratch my head and wonder as I lie in bed,
how did I find the words to rhyme and will there be new poems of
mine?
Gone is my imagination and I can't find an explanation.
I wonder if I'm being led to give this up and read instead.

Printed in Great Britain
by Amazon